ETERNAL SECURITY OR ETERNAL DANGER?

A Biblical Examination of "Once Saved, Always Saved"

Anthony V. Johnson

Eternal Security or Eternal Danger?
A Biblical Examination of "Once Saved, Always Saved"
Copyright © 2026 by Anthony V. Johnson

Requests for information should be addressed to:

Anthony V. Johnson
P.O. Box 450034, Atlanta, Georgia 31145
Email: contact@anthonyvjohnson.com

ISBN: 979-8-9862313-4-1

ACKNOWLEDGMENTS

First and foremost, to my Lord and Savior Jesus Christ—my constant guide, my refuge, and my strength. Your faithfulness has carried me through every trial, and Your Word promises, "I will never leave you nor forsake you" (Hebrews 13:5). Because of Your grace, I press forward with hope, joy, and unwavering anticipation of the day You will say, "Well done, my good and faithful servant" (Matthew 25:21).

To my beloved wife, Deborah, whose love, encouragement, and quiet strength inspire me daily. Your faith, patience, and selflessness reflect the heart of a true Woman of God, and I am forever blessed to walk this journey with you.

To my father, my hero, whose courage and dedication shaped the man I am today. I remember the early mornings at the sound of the doorbell, marking his return from yet another deployment. Resting now at Arlington National Cemetery, his legacy of honor and service continues to guide and inspire me.

To my mother, whose gentle and steadfast love remains a guiding light, even in her absence. Her memory fuels my commitment to live a life of purpose and integrity.

To Pastor Mirek and Linda Hufton of World Harvest Church (Roswell, Georgia), for their tireless leadership and devotion to guiding thousands into a closer walk with Christ. They continue to send 62 or more mission teams worldwide each year saving souls by the thousands.

To Pastor Willie Russell and Flossie, whose hands-on ministry in South Africa reminds us that faith without action is incomplete.

To Apostle Fritz Musser of Tabernacle International Church (Lawrenceville, Georgia), for equipping the saints and fostering sound teaching and leadership.

Finally, to all who have walked alongside me—family, friends, mentors, and fellow laborers in the faith—your encouragement, prayers, and example have shaped this journey. May God's blessings return to you a hundredfold.

PREFACE

Few doctrines have offered as much comfort—or generated as much controversy—as the teaching commonly known as "Once Saved, Always Saved."

For many believers, this doctrine provides deep assurance. It proclaims that salvation, once truly received, can never be lost. It emphasizes God's faithfulness, the sufficiency of Christ's atonement, and the power of divine grace to preserve His people.

Those are precious truths.

And yet, Scripture also contains sober warnings—warnings addressed not to unbelievers, but to those who have tasted the grace of God. The New Testament repeatedly calls believers to remain, to endure, to hold fast, to persevere. It warns against falling away, drifting, and departing from the living God.

How are we to reconcile these themes?

This book was not written to provoke division, nor to diminish the comfort of the gospel. It was written because the biblical warnings deserve to be taken seriously. If Scripture repeatedly cautions believers about the danger of falling away, we must ask whether those warnings describe a real possibility or merely a hypothetical one.

The goal of this work is not to attack brothers and sisters in Christ who hold to the perseverance of the saints. Many who affirm that doctrine are sincere, godly, and deeply committed to Scripture. Rather, this book seeks to examine the issue carefully—biblically, historically, and theologically.

Part I establishes a foundational understanding of salvation as presented in Scripture.
Part II presents the Reformed doctrine of perseverance fairly and in its strongest form.
Part III evaluates the warning passages of Scripture and the testimony of the early church to determine whether unconditional eternal security reflects the full counsel of God.

My conviction, after careful study, is that Scripture does not support the popular formulation of "Once Saved, Always Saved." Salvation is entirely by grace. It is secure in Christ. But the New Testament consistently presents that salvation as something believers must continue in by faith.

The aim of this book is not to unsettle tender consciences, but to guard against presumption. Assurance is biblical. Complacency is not.

If this work leads readers back to Scripture with renewed seriousness— and deeper commitment to abiding in Christ—its purpose will have been fulfilled.

- This book is part of an ongoing effort to examine core Christian doctrines in light of Scripture.
- Future volumes will examine related themes.

TABLE OF CONTENTS

INTRODUCTION

For some years now, I have found myself troubled by the doctrine commonly referred to as *"Once Saved, Always Saved."* This concern arises because, at face value, the doctrine appears to directly contradict what I read in Scripture. Of course, if the doctrine of *Once Saved, Always Saved* is, in fact, true, then all is well. Eternity is not theoretical. Every day, thousands step into eternity. Some suddenly. Some quietly. Some confident. And some unprepared.

Few theological questions are more serious than this one: Is salvation permanently secured by a past decision, or does Scripture call believers to endure in faith until the end?

This book was not written to stir controversy. It was written out of concern. Concern for clarity. Concern for the church. Concern for souls.

The doctrine often summarized as "Once Saved, Always Saved" has become deeply embedded in modern evangelical thought. For many believers, it is assumed rather than examined. It is repeated more often than it is studied. Yet Scripture contains both profound assurances and sobering warnings. Jesus promises eternal life to His sheep. But He also warns that not everyone who calls Him "Lord" will enter the kingdom.

Salvation lies at the very heart of the Christian faith. Yet many within the evangelical church firmly believe that a person who has come to faith in Christ is eternally secure. This doctrine is often presented as an unshakable promise—one that, once received, can never be lost.

Paul exults that nothing can separate us from the love of God. But he also warns believers to continue in His goodness lest they be cut off. The writer of Hebrews comforts suffering Christians. But he also warns of falling away. The question is not whether Scripture contains assurance. It clearly does. The question is whether Scripture presents that assurance as unconditional, irrespective of continued faith — or as covenantal, relational, and enduring.

However, when Scripture is examined carefully, this belief raises significant questions and concerns. Does Scripture truly teach that a person, once saved, can never lose his or her salvation, regardless of lifestyle or beliefs? Or does this doctrine diminish the urgency and seriousness of the Christian faith and the call to salvation?

This book argues that the New Testament consistently calls believers to perseverance.

Salvation begins by grace, continues by grace, and is completed by grace. But grace does not eliminate the call to remain.

Why This Matters

This issue is not merely theological. It is pastoral. If final salvation cannot be forfeited under any circumstance, then the warning passages must be reinterpreted as either hypothetical or descriptive of those who were never truly saved.

But if those warnings are genuine — if they are addressed to real believers — then they must be taken seriously. How we answer this question affects:

- How we preach repentance
- How we counsel the drifting believer

- How we warn the complacent
- How we understand assurance

In some church contexts, salvation is reduced to a moment — a prayer, a card, and an aisle walked. After that moment, the matter is considered permanently settled. But the New Testament presents salvation as a living union with Christ.

Jesus speaks of abiding. Paul speaks of continuing. Hebrews speaks of holding fast. These are relational terms. The gospel does not merely invite a decision; it calls for discipleship.

In this book, we will explore these crucial questions by examining the foundational Scriptures that proponents of *Once Saved, Always Saved* use to support their position. We will also examine Scriptures that appear to challenge this doctrine.

To begin, we will explore why salvation is necessary and consider the nature of salvation itself, highlighting the tension between God's promises of security and His call to perseverance and holiness. Furthermore, we will examine the views of the early Church Fathers within their historical context, including their understanding of the possibility of apostasy. We will also consider whether salvation should be understood as a one-time event or as a lifelong journey of faith.

A Balanced Approach

This book does not seek to diminish grace. It affirms without hesitation:

- Salvation is initiated by God
- Justification is by grace through faith
- No one earns eternal life

But it also affirms that Scripture repeatedly calls believers to endure. The early church understood salvation as a journey of faithfulness empowered by grace.

The Reformers emphasized the preserving power of God. Modern evangelicalism has often emphasized assurance — sometimes at the expense of warning. Each stream contains important truths. This book seeks to listen carefully to all of Scripture, allowing both promise and warning to stand.

What This Book Is Not

This book is not an attack on those who hold to eternal security. Many sincere, faithful believers hold that position. It is not an attempt to produce anxiety or spiritual instability. It is not an argument for works-based righteousness. Rather, it is a call to reexamine Scripture carefully and honestly. If Scripture teaches perseverance as necessary, then perseverance must be preached. If Scripture warns believers of falling away, those warnings must not be softened.

The Structure of This Book

The chapters that follow will:

- Examine the Reformed doctrine of perseverance
- Evaluate key warning passages
- Consider the testimony of the early church
- Address common objections
- Reflect on the implications for the modern church

The goal is not to unsettle faithful believers. The goal is to remove false assurance where it exists and strengthen true assurance where it belongs — in a present, living relationship with Christ.

The Center of the Matter

Salvation is secure in Christ. But Scripture consistently calls believers to remain in Him.

The issue before us is not whether God is faithful. He is.

The issue is whether Scripture teaches that continued faith matters. If it does, then the church must proclaim it clearly. Eternity is not theoretical. It is approaching.

And what we believe about salvation shapes how we live until we meet the Lord. Getting this right is critical. Our eternal destiny depends on it.

PART 1
FOUNDATIONS OF SALVATION

CHAPTER ONE

THE HUMAN CONDITION AND OUR NEED FOR REDEMPTION

Before addressing the question of eternal security, we must begin with a more fundamental question:

Why is salvation necessary at all?

Scripture teaches that humanity was created by God and for God. Genesis 1–2 describes a world formed by divine command and declared good. God created man from the dust of the earth and breathed into him the breath of life, and man became a living soul. Adam was given stewardship over creation and placed in the Garden of Eden. Eve was formed as his companion, and together they lived in fellowship with their Creator.

Yet this fellowship was not without moral boundary. God commanded Adam not to eat from the tree of the knowledge of good and evil, warning that disobedience would result in death.

Genesis 3 records the turning point of human history.

The serpent—identified in Revelation 12:9 as "that old serpent, called the Devil, and Satan"—approached Eve with subtlety. He questioned God's word and introduced doubt: "Yea, hath God said…?" (Genesis 3:1). What began as deception culminated in disobedience. Eve ate of the forbidden fruit and gave also unto Adam, and he ate. Through this act, sin entered the human experience.

The consequence was immediate spiritual separation. Shame replaced innocence. Fear replaced fellowship. Humanity's relationship with God was fractured. Isaiah later summarizes this condition: "Your iniquities have separated between you and your God" (Isaiah 59:2, KJV).

The effects of Adam's disobedience extended beyond Eden. Scripture teaches that sin spread to all humanity. Paul writes, "By one man sin entered into the world, and death by sin; and so death passed upon all men" (Romans 5:12, KJV).

Every person is born into this fallen condition.

We are not sinners merely because we sin; we sin because we are sinners. Romans 3:10–12 declares, "There is none righteous, no, not one." Left to ourselves, we cannot restore what was broken. No moral effort, religious ritual, or human achievement can undo the separation caused by sin.

Because sin is universal, salvation is necessary.

Under the old covenant, God instituted a sacrificial system. The shedding of blood symbolized atonement and pointed toward the seriousness of sin. Yet those sacrifices were temporary and repetitive, unable to permanently remove guilt.

They anticipated something greater.

Hebrews 9:12–14 declares that Christ entered once into the holy place "by His own blood," having obtained eternal redemption. Unlike the blood of animals, His sacrifice was sufficient. At the cross, Jesus bore the penalty of sin and provided reconciliation between God and humanity.

Through His death and resurrection, He accomplished what no human effort could achieve.

Salvation is therefore not self-improvement. It is divine rescue.

And this rescue is found in Christ alone. Jesus declared, "I am the way, the truth, and the life: no man cometh unto the Father, but by me" (John 14:6, KJV). The apostles affirmed the same exclusivity: "Neither is there salvation in any other: for there is none other name under heaven given among men, whereby we must be saved" (Acts 4:12, KJV). Scripture does not present salvation as one option among many. It presents Christ as the only mediator between God and man.

Romans 6:23 summarizes the contrast: "For the wages of sin is death; but the gift of God is eternal life through Jesus Christ our Lord."

Every human being stands in need of this gift. Without it, we remain under the sentence of death. With it, we receive forgiveness, reconciliation, and eternal life.

To discuss perseverance, assurance, or eternal security without first understanding the depth of human fallenness would be premature. Salvation is not optional—it is essential.

All people are born in sin. None are inherently righteous. None can save themselves.

Redemption is not a theological accessory. It is the only remedy for the human condition.

CHAPTER TWO

SALVATION: A COMPREHENSIVE UNDERSTANDING

We have seen how sin entered the world, and we now understand why salvation is necessary. With this foundation in place, we can explore what salvation truly entails.

Salvation involves deliverance from sin and its consequences, and it can be obtained only through Jesus Christ. Scripture declares, *"Neither is there salvation in any other: for there is none other name under heaven given among men, whereby we must be saved"* (Acts 4:12). Salvation is made possible through the life, death, and resurrection of Jesus Christ.

When a person receives salvation through Jesus Christ, the believer is declared *justified* before God (Romans 3:24). The believer is also being *sanctified* through the ongoing process of being made holy (Hebrews 10:14). Ultimately, the believer will experience *glorification*—the final perfection of the believer in eternity (Philippians 3:21).

When a believer is saved, he or she is reconciled to God, freed from the penalty of sin, and granted eternal life. Scripture affirms this promise: *"For God so loved the world, that He gave His only begotten Son, that whosoever believeth in Him should not perish, but have everlasting life"* (John 3:16).

CHAPTER THREE

RECEIVING GOD'S GIFT: HOW SALVATION IS OBTAINED

We now understand why salvation is necessary and what salvation entails. We can now turn our attention to how a person is saved.

First, it must be clearly stated that salvation cannot be obtained by attending church or by becoming a member of a religious organization. Nor can a person be saved without understanding what salvation truly means. Dedicating or baptizing a baby does not constitute salvation. Likewise, being born into a family that attends a particular church or follows a specific religious tradition does not make a person saved.

Additionally, attending a church service in which a pastor announces that "the doors of the church are open" does not equate to salvation. This phrase typically refers to church membership, not conversion. Salvation does not come through church attendance or organizational affiliation.

In many Christian churches, the term *"the sinner's prayer"* is commonly used. While the phrase itself does not appear in Scripture, the elements often included in such a prayer are biblical requirements for salvation.

Romans 10:9–10 states: *"That if thou shalt confess with thy mouth the Lord Jesus, and shalt believe in thine heart that God hath raised him from the dead, thou shalt be saved. For with the heart man believeth unto righteousness; and with the mouth confession is made unto salvation."*

From this passage, we see several key elements. First, there is confession—an open acknowledgment of Jesus Christ as Lord. Second, there is belief in the heart that God raised Jesus from the dead. This belief encompasses faith in Jesus' virgin birth, His sacrificial death on the cross for our sins, and His bodily resurrection on the third day.

However, salvation involves more than intellectual assent. A person must first recognize that he or she is a sinner in need of salvation. Romans 3:23 declares, *"For all have sinned, and come short of the glory of God."* This recognition leads to confession of sin. First John 1:9–10 states:

"If we confess our sins, he is faithful and just to forgive us our sins, and to cleanse us from all unrighteousness."

Salvation also requires repentance. Acts 3:19 says, *"Repent therefore, and be converted, that your sins may be blotted out."* Repentance involves genuine sorrow for sin and a deliberate turning away from sinful behavior. Jesus Himself warned in Luke 13:3, *"Except ye repent, ye shall all likewise perish."* Heaven rejoices over true repentance, as stated in Luke 15:7.

True repentance includes several components: acknowledgment of sin (Psalm 51:3–4), turning away from sin (Isaiah 55:7), godly sorrow (2 Corinthians 7:10), faith in God's mercy (Luke 18:13–14), and a changed life evidenced by righteous actions (Matthew 3:8; Acts 26:20).

In summary, salvation involves a transformed heart, genuine sorrow over sin, and a commitment to walk in obedience to God. This aligns with God's will and opens the way for forgiveness, restoration, and salvation.

Below is a commonly used example of the *"sinner's prayer,"* which reflects these biblical principles:

"Dear God, I know that I am a sinner. I repent of my sins and ask for Your forgiveness. I believe that Jesus Christ died for my sins on the cross at Calvary and that You raised Him from the grave on the third day. Lord Jesus, I ask You to come into my heart and be my Lord and Savior. I choose to trust You and follow You from this day forward. Guide my life and help me to do Your will. In Jesus' name I pray, Amen."

Another aspect of salvation is the public declaration of faith through water baptism. Jesus said in Mark 16:16, *"He that believeth and is baptized shall be saved; but he that believeth not shall be damned."* In Acts 2:38, Peter declared, *"Repent, and be baptized every one of you in the name of Jesus Christ for the remission of sins."*

Biblical baptism requires full immersion in water, symbolizing Christ's death, burial, and resurrection. Scripture provides no example of baptism by sprinkling; this practice arises from human tradition rather than biblical instruction. As with salvation, baptism must be a conscious and informed decision made between the individual and God.

Beyond conversion and baptism, Scripture emphasizes obedience and perseverance. Jesus said in John 14:15, *"If ye love me, keep my commandments."* Philippians 2:12 exhorts believers to *"work out your own salvation with fear and trembling."*

It is also important to address the sincerity of belief. It is possible for someone to pray the sinner's prayer without genuine faith. For example, I once prayed such a prayer under pressure as a young man in the Army, despite not actively following Christ at the time. Though the words were spoken, true commitment was lacking. This demonstrates that salvation is not about reciting words, but about genuine belief and surrender of the heart.

Similarly, individuals may respond to an altar call for salvation due to pressure from a friend or relative rather than true conviction. This underscores the importance of discipleship and follow-up after a profession of faith. Even so, God can use these moments to plant seeds that later produce genuine faith.

Humility is another essential element of salvation. Walking in obedience requires a humble heart. Second Chronicles 7:14 declares, *"If my people… shall humble themselves, and pray, and seek my face, and turn from their wicked ways; then will I hear from heaven, and will forgive their sin."*

In summary, salvation involves recognizing one's sinful condition, believing in Jesus Christ as Lord and Savior, repenting of sin, confessing faith openly, being baptized as an act of obedience, walking in humility, living out one's faith, and persevering until the end. While believers may still stumble, Scripture assures us that forgiveness remains available through repentance (1 John 1:9).

Now that we understand why salvation is necessary, what it entails, and how it is received, we can turn our attention to the next critical question: **Can salvation be lost?**

CHAPTER FOUR

THE NATURE OF SALVATION: IS IT A ONE-TIME DECISION OR A LIFELONG JOURNEY?

When considering the doctrine of *Once Saved, Always Saved*, a major point of contention is whether salvation is a one-time decision or a lifelong journey. Proponents of this doctrine argue that once a person is saved, salvation can never be lost—regardless of how one lives afterward. This raises an essential question: *Is salvation a single event, or is it an ongoing process?*

Scripture shows that salvation begins with **justification**, a one-time declaration of righteousness through faith. Romans 5:1 states, *"Therefore being justified by faith, we have peace with God through our Lord Jesus Christ."* However, salvation continues through **sanctification**, which involves a lifelong process of being conformed to the image of Christ.

Philippians 2:12–13 declares:
"Wherefore, my beloved… work out your own salvation with fear and trembling. For it is God which worketh in you both to will and to do of his good pleasure."

Notice that believers are instructed to *work out* their salvation. This instruction directly challenges the notion that salvation is merely a one-time decision with no ongoing responsibility.

Sanctification involves both divine empowerment and human responsibility. While God works within the believer, the believer must actively pursue holiness and obedience. Daily, we are called to align our thoughts, actions, and desires with God's will.

The Holy Spirit plays a crucial role in this process. He convicts us of sin, guides us into truth, and empowers us to live godly lives. This transformation is gradual and often includes trials, discipline, and perseverance. As discussed in my book *PSYOPS: The Spiritual Battle for Your Mind and Your Soul! – Countdown to Eternity*, believers face continual spiritual opposition from the devil, the flesh, and the world. Living a holy and upright life is not easy—it is a lifelong pursuit.

Repentance is also an ongoing posture of the heart. While repentance often begins at conversion, it does not end there. Believers must continually depend on God's grace, confess sin, and walk in obedience. Jesus emphasized this daily commitment in Luke 9:23: *"If any man will come after me, let him deny himself, and take up his cross daily, and follow me."*

Repentance, therefore, is not a one-time act but a lifestyle. It requires humility, sensitivity to the conviction of the Holy Spirit, and a teachable spirit. No believer ever "arrives" at a place where growth is no longer necessary.

Perseverance is another essential element of salvation. Jesus declared in Matthew 24:13, *"But he that shall endure unto the end, the same shall be saved."* Salvation is not only about how one begins the Christian life, but also about how one finishes it.

The apostle Paul provides a powerful example of perseverance when he wrote, *"I have fought a good fight, I have finished my course, I have kept the faith"* (2 Timothy 4:7). Likewise, Hebrews 12:1–2 exhorts believers to run the race with endurance, laying aside sin and keeping their eyes fixed on Jesus, *"the author and finisher of our faith."*

The Christian life is not a sprint—it is a marathon. It demands endurance through trials, temptations, and hardships. Salvation begins with justification, but it continues through sanctification. Repentance, obedience, and perseverance are not optional add-ons; they are essential aspects of the journey.

We are called to endure to the end, remaining faithful and relying on God's strength. As Scripture clearly states, *"He that shall endure unto the end, the same shall be saved"* (Matthew 24:13).

PART II
THE REFORMED DOCTRINE OF PERSEVERANCE

CHAPTER FIVE

THE CASE FOR "ONCE SAVED, ALWAYS SAVED": CALVIN, DORT, AND THE DOCTRINE OF PERSEVERANCE

The doctrine commonly summarized as "Once Saved, Always Saved" is most fully articulated within Reformed theology under the title *the Perseverance of the Saints*. While the slogan can oversimplify the doctrine, the theological claim itself is precise: all who are truly regenerated by God will certainly persevere in faith until final glorification.

This conviction is rooted most clearly in the theology of John Calvin and was later codified at the Synod of Dort (1618–1619)[1] According to this tradition, salvation is not merely initiated by grace—it is sustained and completed by that same sovereign grace. It is believed that those who ultimately fall away were never truly regenerated, even if they once appeared to believe.

Before evaluating this doctrine critically, it is essential to present it in its strongest form.

---

[1] Synod of Dort, *The Canons of Dort* (1619).

1. John Calvin: Effectual Calling and the "Golden Chain"

At the heart of Calvin's theology is the conviction that salvation belongs entirely to God. Human beings do not cooperate with grace in a way that determines its final outcome; rather, grace itself produces the response it requires.

Calvin frequently appealed to Romans 8:30, often called the "golden chain" of redemption:

"Moreover whom He predestined, these He also called; whom He called, these He also justified; and whom He justified, these He also glorified."[2]

In his *Institutes of the Christian Religion*, Calvin argued that this sequence is unbreakable.[3] Those whom God predestines are effectually called. Those called are justified. Those justified are glorified. There is no loss between the links of this chain. The certainty of glorification rests not on human constancy, but on divine purpose.

For Calvin, effectual calling guarantees perseverance. If salvation originates in God's eternal decree and is applied through the inward work of the Spirit, then its completion cannot ultimately depend upon fluctuating human faithfulness.[4]

---

[2] Romans 8:30 (NKJV).

[3] John Calvin, *Institutes of the Christian Religion*, ed. John T. McNeill, trans. Ford Lewis Battles (Philadelphia: Westminster Press, 1960), 3.21–24.

[4] Ibid., 3.24.6.

Calvin did not deny that believers struggle. He acknowledged doubt, temptation, and even grievous sin. Yet he distinguished between temporary lapses and final apostasy. The elect may stumble, but they will not finally be lost. God preserves them.[5]

In this framework, biblical warnings function as instruments of perseverance. God uses exhortations and cautions to keep His people vigilant. The warnings are real—but they are means by which God secures perseverance, not indications that salvation can be forfeited.

2. The Synod of Dort: A Formal Definition of Perseverance

The Synod of Dort (1618–1619) convened to respond to the Remonstrant challenge to Reformed theology. Its conclusions were codified in what later became known as the Five Points of Calvinism.[6]

The Fifth Head of Doctrine addresses perseverance directly. It teaches that those whom God has chosen and effectually called are preserved by His power so that they will certainly continue in faith to the end.[7] Though believers may fall into serious sin, they will not finally fall from grace.

Dort carefully distinguished between two categories:

- **True believers**, who are inwardly regenerated and will persevere.
- **Temporary believers**, who may appear converted for a time but lack true saving faith.

---

[5] Ibid., 3.24.7–8.

[6] Synod of Dort, *Canons of Dort*, Heads of Doctrine I–V.

[7] Ibid., Fifth Head of Doctrine, Articles 3–8.

When such individuals fall away, their departure reveals their original condition. Their faith was not the fruit of regeneration but of temporary conviction or external participation.[8]

Thus, perseverance is not grounded in human determination but in divine preservation. The believer continues because God continues His saving work.

3. Reformed Interpretations of Warning Passages

Critics of perseverance theology often appeal to New Testament warnings that appear to describe genuine believers falling away. Among the most frequently cited are:

- Hebrews 6:4–6
- Hebrews 10:26–29
- 2 Peter 2:20–22
- John 15:1–6
- Romans 11:17–22

Reformed theologians generally respond in three ways.

1. Warnings as Means of Grace

The warnings are real and serious, but they function instrumentally. God uses them to keep true believers from apostasy. The elect heed the warnings; those without saving faith disregard them.

2. Apparent Believers

Some individuals participate outwardly in the Christian community and experience significant spiritual exposure yet lack true regeneration.

---

[8] Ibid., Fifth Head of Doctrine, Article 9.

When they fall away, their departure demonstrates that their faith was temporary rather than saving.

3. Temporary or Non-Saving Faith

Reformed theology distinguishes between genuine saving faith and temporary faith. Temporary faith may include intellectual assent, emotional response, and even moral reform. But it does not include the inward renewal produced by the Holy Spirit.[9]

This framework preserves both the certainty of God's promises and the seriousness of biblical warnings.

4. A Brief Consideration of Key Texts

Several warning passages use language that appears strong and experiential.

Hebrews 6 describes those who were "once enlightened," who "tasted the heavenly gift," and who became "partakers" of the Holy Spirit. The word translated "partakers" (*metochos*) denotes a sharer or participant.[10] Reformed interpreters argue that such participation may refer to covenantal exposure rather than regeneration.

Hebrews 10:29 speaks of one who was "sanctified" by the blood of the covenant yet later treats that blood as unholy. The verb *hagiazo* means "to sanctify" or "to set apart."[11] Reformed readings often understand this sanctification in covenantal or external terms rather than as definitive inward renewal.

---

[9] Calvin, *Institutes*, 3.2.11.

[10] Hebrews 6:4; cf. Hebrews 3:1, 14 (NKJV).

[11] Hebrews 10:29; cf. Hebrews 10:10, 14 (NKJV).

Similarly, 2 Peter 2:20 describes those who escaped the world's corruption through the "knowledge" (*epignosis*, full or experiential knowledge) of Jesus Christ, yet became entangled again.[12] Debate centers on whether this knowledge implies regeneration or significant but temporary spiritual experience.

The interpretive question, therefore, does not rest on vocabulary alone but on broader theological commitments concerning election, grace, and perseverance.

5. Core Theological Claims of Perseverance

At its foundation, the Reformed doctrine of perseverance rests on several affirmations:

- God's grace is sovereign from beginning to end.
- Salvation is initiated, sustained, and completed by God.
- True believers persevere because God preserves them.
- Those who fall away reveal that they were never truly regenerate.
- Biblical warnings function as means of spiritual vigilance, not threats to the elect.

In this system, assurance is grounded in God's unchanging decree rather than in the believer's fluctuating experience.

---

[12] 2 Peter 2:20 (NKJV).

6. Preparing for Evaluation

The Calvin/Dort position presents a coherent and internally consistent theological framework. It takes seriously God's sovereignty and the certainty of His promises.

Yet the warning passages remain sobering. They describe real consequences, real apostasies, and real exhortations to continue in faith.

The question that follows—and which the remainder of this book will examine—is whether the Reformed explanation sufficiently accounts for the plain force of these warnings.

To evaluate that question fairly, we must first understand the doctrine of perseverance in its strongest form. Only then can we consider whether Scripture allows for the possibility that a true believer might finally fall away.

CHAPTER SIX

ETERNAL SECURITY: THEOLOGICAL REFLECTIONS FROM THE EARLY CHURCH FATHERS

In this chapter, we will examine the writings of early Christian theologians and discover that their writings emphasize perseverance and vigilance in ways that do not reflect later formulations of unconditional eternity security. . Church Fathers such as Ignatius of Antioch[13], Clement of Rome[14], Polycarp[15], Athanasius[16], and Augustine[17] emphasized perseverance, faithfulness, and vigilance, while warning against falling away from the faith. Their writings reflect a consistent historical understanding that salvation requires ongoing commitment rather than passive assurance.

Ignatius of Antioch, a prominent bishop and martyr, stressed the necessity of steadfastness in the Christian life and warned believers against complacency. He urged Christians to remain faithful to Christ

---

[13] Ignatius of Antioch, *Letter to the Ephesians*, in *The Apostolic Fathers*, ed. Bart D. Ehrman (Cambridge, MA: Harvard University Press, 2003), 48:2.

[14] Clement of Rome, *First Letter to the Corinthians*, in *The Apostolic Fathers*, ed. Bart D. Ehrman, 42:1–5.

[15] Polycarp, *Letter to the Philippians*, in *The Apostolic Fathers*, ed. Bart D. Ehrman, 67:1–2.

[16] Athanasius, *On the Incarnation*, trans. A Religious of C.S.M.V. (Crestwood, NY: St. Vladimir's Seminary Press, 1996), 54.

[17] Augustine of Hippo, *On Grace and Free Will*, in *The Works of Saint Augustine*, trans. A. Cleveland Coxe (New York: Christian Literature Company, 1887), Book II, Ch. 10.

until the end. In his *Letter to the Ephesians*, Ignatius wrote that it is not enough merely to be called Christians, but to live as such in reality. He warned that some profess Christ with their words but deny Him by their actions, concluding that such individuals do not have the seed of God within them[18]. Ignatius clearly understood salvation as requiring a life aligned with one's profession of faith.

Clement of Rome likewise emphasized endurance and obedience in his *Letter to the Corinthians*. He exhorted believers to put aside arrogance, foolish anger, and pride, and instead walk in humility[19]. Clement viewed salvation as a dynamic relationship that requires continual faithfulness, not a static condition guaranteed regardless of one's conduct.

Polycarp of Smyrna, a disciple of the apostle John, also warned believers against falling away. In his *Letter to the Philippians*, he encouraged Christians to serve the Lord in fear and truth abandoning deceit, error, and empty talk. Polycarp's teachings echoed New Testament warnings concerning complacency and false teachers, reinforcing the call to perseverance.

Athanasius, a defender of orthodox Christian doctrine, addressed the tension between divine sovereignty and human responsibility. While affirming God's power to preserve the faithful, he also emphasized the believer's responsibility to remain in Christ[20]. In *On the Incarnation*,

---

[18] Ignatius, *Letter to the Ephesians*, 12:2–3.

[19] Clement of Rome, *First Letter to the Corinthians*, 32:1–3.

[20] Athanasius, *On the Incarnation*, 54–55.

Athanasius highlighted the transformative nature of salvation and the believer's obligation to resist sin, underscoring that salvation involves an active, ongoing response to God's grace.

Augustine of Hippo also contributed significantly to the discussion of salvation and perseverance. Although Augustine strongly emphasized divine grace, he nonetheless acknowledged the reality and danger of apostasy[21]. In his writings against the Pelagians—who denied humanity's need for divine grace—Augustine argued that while God provides the grace necessary for salvation, believers must cooperate with that grace through faith and obedience. Augustine acknowledged that some who appear to believe may later fall away, while also emphasizing God's sovereign gift of perseverance. In summary, the early Church Fathers consistently taught that salvation requires vigilance, faithfulness, and perseverance. They did not view salvation as a single, irreversible event, but as a lifelong journey demanding endurance. This perspective aligns with Scripture's repeated warnings against falling away. Hebrews 3:12–13 cautions: *"Take heed, brethren, lest there be in any of you an evil heart of unbelief, in departing from the living God."*[22]

Similarly, Scripture speaks plainly of a future "falling away" from the faith. Second Thessalonians 2:3 states: *"Let no man deceive you by any means: for that day shall not come, except there come a falling away first.*[23]*"* This passage implies that some who once professed faith will later turn away.

---

[21] Augustine, *On Grace and Free Will*, Book II, Ch. 10; *Confessions*, Book IX, Ch. 10.

[22] Hebrews 3:12–13 (NKJV).

[23] 2 Thessalonians 2:3 (NKJV).

The teachings of the early Church Fathers consistently called believers to endurance, emphasizing that faith must be accompanied by obedience and perseverance. Notably, the doctrine of *Once Saved, Always Saved* is absent from early Christian writings. Instead, the emphasis is placed on remaining faithful to Christ and guarding against spiritual complacency.

While the writings of the early Church Fathers are not authoritative in the same way as Scripture, they provide valuable historical insight into how the earliest Christians understood salvation. Ultimately, Scripture alone is our final authority, and any teaching that contradicts it must be rejected.[24]

Methodological Clarification

This study does not claim that the early Church Fathers articulated the later theological categories of either Reformed or Arminian systems. Rather, their writings are examined to determine how they described salvation, perseverance, and the possibility of falling away in their own historical contexts. Because patristic theology developed prior to the precise formulations of the Reformation era, their language is analyzed descriptively rather than retroactively forced into later confessional frameworks. Scripture remains the final authority, and historical theology serves as illumination, not norm.

---

[24] 2 Timothy 3:16–17 (NKJV).

CHAPTER SEVEN

THE DANGER OF PRESUMPTION: GRACE VS. LICENSE

As a result of the price Jesus paid for us on the cross at Calvary, believers have entered into a new covenant of grace. Grace refers to the unmerited favor of God—extended to us despite our sin, imperfections, and unworthiness. God's grace cannot be earned. Scripture declares in Ephesians 2:8–9, *"For by grace are ye saved through faith; and that not of yourselves: it is the gift of God: Not of works, lest any man should boast."*

However, God's grace is never intended to be an excuse for sin. In Romans 6, the apostle Paul confronts this very misunderstanding: *"What shall we say then? Shall we continue in sin, that grace may abound? God forbid. How shall we, that are dead to sin, live any longer therein?"* (Romans 6:1–2).

The doctrine of *Once Saved, Always Saved* often fosters spiritual complacency and moral indifference. If a person believes that eternity in heaven is guaranteed regardless of lifestyle, what incentive remains to pursue holiness or Christlikeness? Under this doctrine, the primary distinction between a professing Christian and an unbeliever may amount to nothing more than whether one has prayed a prayer.

Some argue that while salvation cannot be lost, only one's *rewards* in heaven are affected by earthly conduct. There is some truth as pertains to rewards, but only if the person is genuinely saved. Scripture does teach that believers will receive rewards according to their faithfulness and obedience.

Jesus addressed the issue of reward in Matthew 6:1, warning against self-promotion: *"Take heed that ye do not your alms before men, to be seen of them: otherwise ye have no reward of your Father which is in heaven."* Acts of generosity done for public praise receive no heavenly reward. In contrast, Matthew 6:3–4 teaches that acts done in secret will be rewarded openly by God.

Scripture also promises reward for enduring persecution. Matthew 5:12 declares, *"Rejoice, and be exceeding glad: for great is your reward in heaven."* Luke 6:23 echoes this same truth.

The Bible further teaches that a believer's works will be tested. First Corinthians 3:13–14 states: *"Every man's work shall be made manifest… If any man's work abide… he shall receive a reward."* This passage emphasizes accountability, not license.

Scripture also speaks of rewards described as *crowns*. Second Timothy 4:8 refers to the crown of righteousness. Revelation 2:10 mentions the crown of life, promised to those who remain faithful unto death. First Peter 5:1–4 describes the crown of glory, given to faithful shepherds of God's people.

The existence of heavenly rewards does not negate the possibility of forfeiting salvation. These rewards are reserved for those who endure to the end and remain faithful.

Unfortunately, the doctrine of *Once Saved, Always Saved* often serves well for those pastors and teachers who avoid preaching on sin, repentance, holiness, and the fear of God. Instead, many emphasize that "all is well" while promoting financial sowing as the means to personal prosperity. The eternal destiny of the soul is rarely addressed, while material gain becomes the central message.

I previously mentioned a pastor who publicly shamed his congregation over financial giving, even calling out those who gave large sums. His concern was not the condition of their souls, but the contents of their wallets. My wife and I left that church immediately after hearing him make two disturbing statements. First, he claimed he could not distinguish his wife's voice from the voice of God. Second, while recounting his time at a former church, he stated that members were expected to mortgage their homes and give the money to him. When they refused, he angrily concluded, *"That twelve million dollars… that was supposed to be my money!"* That was the last day we ever attended that ministry.

Scripture repeatedly warns against presumption. First Corinthians 10:12 states, *"Wherefore let him that thinketh he standeth take heed lest he fall."* A lack of commitment to holiness reflects a dangerous presumption upon God's grace and undermines the transforming power of salvation.

Grace does not excuse sin—it trains us to reject it. Titus 2:11–12 declares, *"For the grace of God that bringeth salvation hath appeared to all men, teaching us that, denying ungodliness and worldly lusts, we should live soberly, righteously, and godly, in this present world."* We are called to live holy lives, walk in obedience, and humble ourselves before God.

As Scripture reminds us, *"The fear of the LORD is the beginning of wisdom: and the knowledge of the holy is understanding"* (Proverbs 9:10).

CHAPTER EIGHT

GOD'S FAITHFULNESS VS. HUMAN RESPONSIBILITY

A clear tension exists in Scripture between the faithfulness of God and the responsibility of believers to remain faithful. God's promises are unwavering, yet the Bible repeatedly emphasizes the need for vigilance, obedience, and endurance. This theme appears consistently throughout both the Old and New Testaments.

In this chapter, we will examine key biblical passages that highlight God's sovereignty alongside human responsibility within the journey of salvation. We will also consider sobering warnings found in passages such as John 15:6, which states: *If a man abide not in me, he is cast forth as a branch, and is withered; and men gather them, and cast them into the fire, and they are burned.* " Likewise, Matthew 24:13 declares, *"But he that shall endure unto the end, the same shall be saved."*

John 15:6 presents a stark warning through the metaphor of the vine and the branches. A branch that does not remain connected to the vine is cut off, withers, and is ultimately thrown into the fire. This imagery leaves little room for complacency.

The Call to Remain in Christ

The metaphor in John 15 underscores the necessity of abiding in Christ—remaining continually connected to the source of spiritual life. By abiding in Him, believers receive nourishment, strength, and guidance for daily living.

This passage also makes clear that salvation is not automatic or unconditional in its application. Believers bear responsibility to maintain their relationship with Christ through faith and obedience. God graciously provides everything necessary to remain in Him, yet failure to abide results in spiritual separation and judgment.

The Endurance of the Faithful

Matthew 24:13 reinforces the theme of perseverance, particularly in the context of trials and tribulation. While the passage has an immediate prophetic context, the principle applies universally: salvation is not merely about beginning the journey, but about enduring to the end.

Believers are enabled to endure through God's grace and the empowering work of the Holy Spirit. Philippians 2:12–13 instructs us: *"Work out your own salvation with fear and trembling. For it is God which worketh in you both to will and to do of his good pleasure."*

This passage highlights the balance between divine empowerment and human participation in spiritual growth.

The Role of Free Will

Human free will is evident throughout Scripture. God grants each person the ability to choose obedience or disobedience. From the beginning, God placed Adam and Eve in the Garden of Eden and gave them a clear command regarding the tree of the knowledge of good and evil.

Genesis 3:1–3 records the exchange between the serpent and Eve, demonstrating that God's command was clear, yet the choice to obey or disobey remained theirs. God did not force obedience, nor does He do so today.

Throughout Scripture, God issues commands and expectations, yet He allows individuals to choose. With that freedom comes accountability. Disobedience carries consequences, and Scripture never suggests otherwise.

Warnings Against Falling Away

The Bible contains explicit warnings directed toward believers. Hebrews 6:4–6 is among the most sobering:

> *"For it is impossible for those who were once enlightened… if they shall fall away, to renew them again unto repentance."*

This passage warns against the danger of apostasy. It affirms that those who have genuinely experienced the realities of salvation can choose to turn away. While salvation is freely given by grace, Scripture teaches that it must be lived out through continued faith and obedience.

Spiritual Vigilance and Perseverance

Believers are repeatedly warned against spiritual complacency. We face ongoing opposition from the world, the flesh, and the devil. Therefore, vigilance is essential. First Corinthians 10:12 cautions, *"Wherefore let him that thinketh he standeth take heed lest he fall."*

Spiritual vigilance guards against the deceitfulness of sin and the distractions of the world. Perseverance is not optional—it is essential to faithful discipleship.

By remaining in Christ, believers experience the assurance of God's promises and the security found in Him alone. God is faithful, but He calls His people to remain faithful as well.

CHAPTER NINE

PERSEVERANCE OF THE SAINTS: WHAT DOES IT REALLY MEAN?

Perseverance is commonly understood as steadfastness in the face of difficulty. In Scripture, however, perseverance refers not merely to resilience, but to faithful endurance in obedience to God until the end.

The New Testament repeatedly emphasizes the necessity of enduring faith.

Philippians 2:12 instructs believers:

"Work out your own salvation with fear and trembling."

This exhortation is not addressed to unbelievers but to those already identified as "beloved." The command assumes an ongoing responsibility — not to earn salvation, but to live it out reverently and obediently.

Similarly, Jesus declares in Matthew 24:13:

"He that shall endure unto the end, the same shall be saved."

Endurance is presented not as optional but as essential. Salvation, in this context, is associated with continuing fidelity.

These passages challenge any conception of salvation that reduces it to a single past moment detached from ongoing obedience. The Christian life is not sustained by a memory of conversion alone, but by persevering trust in Christ.

Scripture consistently calls God's people to holiness. First Peter 1:16 declares:

"Be ye holy; for I am holy."

This command echoes Leviticus 11:44 and reveals that holiness is not merely aspirational; it is a divine expectation grounded in God's own character.

Ephesians 5:27 further describes the church Christ will present to Himself as:

"a glorious church, not having spot, or wrinkle… holy and without blemish."

The vision is corporate and transformative. Christ is forming a people marked by purification and faithfulness.

Therefore, biblical perseverance cannot be reduced to passive security. It is active, reverent endurance in faith and obedience. It involves:

- Ongoing trust in Christ
- Resistance to sin
- Pursuit of holiness
- Vigilance against unbelief

Perseverance is not complacency; it is covenantal fidelity.

The question that remains, and which must be examined carefully, is whether this perseverance is unconditionally guaranteed for all who have truly believed — or whether Scripture leaves open the possibility that genuine believers may fall away through persistent unbelief.

That question requires further examination of the warning passages themselves.

PART III
THE BIBLICAL WARNINGS AND THE QUESTION OF APOSTASY

CHAPTER TEN

FALLING AWAY: IS IT POSSIBLE TO LOSE SALVATION?

In this chapter, we will examine key Scripture passages commonly used by proponents of the doctrine of *Once Saved, Always Saved,* as well as passages that directly challenge its validity.

The doctrine of *Once Saved, Always Saved* teaches that once a person receives salvation, they can **never** lose it and are guaranteed eternity in heaven. If this doctrine were true—then, admittedly, the matter would be simple. We could all relax.

However, if this doctrine is true, it would also mean that once a person accepts Jesus as Lord and Savior, he or she could live however they please, with no eternal consequences for their choices. That assumption carries serious theological implications. To arrive at the truth, we must examine Scripture carefully—beginning with the passages often cited in support of eternal security.

Scriptures Commonly Used to Support Eternal Security

One frequently cited passage is John 10:28:
"And I give unto them eternal life; and they shall never perish, neither shall any man pluck them out of my hand."

However, this promise cannot be separated from the preceding verse. John 10:27 states:
"My sheep hear my voice, and I know them, and they follow me."

The promise of security in verse 28 applies specifically to **those who hear Christ's voice and follow Him.** It does not apply indiscriminately to those who refuse obedience or disregard His voice. Jesus is speaking of *His sheep*—those who remain in relationship with Him.

Many people claim to be Christians simply because they attend church occasionally or identify with Christianity culturally or through family affiliation. Yet countless individuals who identify as Christians have never cultivated a prayer life, never studied Scripture, and rarely—if ever—attend church. Jesus said His sheep *hear His voice.* That distinction matters.

Another passage often cited is Romans 8:38–39:
"For I am persuaded, that neither death, nor life…nor any other creature, shall be able to separate us from the love of God, which is in Christ Jesus our Lord."

This passage speaks of **God's love,** not an unconditional guarantee of salvation regardless of human response. God loves both the saved and the unsaved. John 3:16 affirms that God loved *the world*—yet belief and obedience remain necessary responses.

Philippians 1:6 is also commonly referenced:
"Being confident of this very thing, that he which hath begun a good work in you will perform it until the day of Jesus Christ."

However, this statement was addressed specifically to *"all the saints in Christ Jesus which are at Philippi, with the bishops and deacons"* (Philippians 1:1). It assumes continued faithfulness, not abandonment of Christ.

Similarly, Hebrews 10:14 states:

"For by one offering he hath perfected forever them that are sanctified."

Sanctification refers to those who are actively set apart for God—not those who return to sin and rebellion.

Scriptures That Challenge the Doctrine of Eternal Security

Ephesians 5:27 describes the church Christ will present to Himself:

"A glorious church, not having spot, or wrinkle…holy and without blemish."

Yet when one observes many churches today, holiness is often absent. Instead, scandals involving money and sexual immorality abound. Sin, repentance, the fear of God, and holiness are rarely addressed. In their place are entertainment, false doctrine, compromise, and acceptance of sinful lifestyles—all in pursuit of popularity and financial gain.

Philippians 2:12 presents a serious challenge to eternal security:

"Work out your own salvation with fear and trembling."

If salvation were irrevocable regardless of behavior, such a command would be unnecessary. Fear and trembling imply responsibility, accountability, and the possibility of loss.

Revelation 3:5 is even more explicit:

"He that overcometh… I will not blot out his name out of the book of life."

This statement clearly implies that names **can** be blotted out. Otherwise, the warning would be meaningless.

Second Peter 2:20–22 offers one of the clearest warnings:

"For if after they have escaped the pollutions of the world through the knowledge of the Lord and Saviour Jesus Christ, they are again entangled therein... the latter end is worse with them than the beginning."

These individuals *knew* Christ and then turned away.

Hebrews 6:4–6 further confirms this reality, describing those who were enlightened, partakers of the Holy Spirit, and yet fell away. Hebrews 10:26–27 warns of willful sin after receiving the knowledge of the truth—resulting not in security, but judgment.

The Most Sobering Warning of All

Matthew 7:21–23 stands as perhaps the most devastating refutation of *Once Saved, Always Saved*:

"Not every one that saith unto me, Lord, Lord, shall enter into the kingdom of heaven..."

These individuals **prophesied**, **cast out demons**, and **performed miracles** in Jesus' name—yet they were rejected. Jesus said, *"I never knew you."* These were not casual believers; they were ministers. And Jesus said *many*, not few, would be rejected.

This passage alone dismantles the notion that profession, spiritual activity, or past experience guarantees eternal life.

The Reality of a Falling Away

Second Thessalonians 2:3 warns that a great falling away would occur before Christ's return. First Timothy 4:1–2 confirms that many will depart from the faith, embracing deception and false doctrine.

What we are witnessing today—the moral collapse, doctrinal compromise, and spiritual corruption within many churches—is evidence that this falling away is already underway.

Jesus warned in Matthew 15:8–9 that people would honor Him with their lips while their hearts remained far from Him. Blind leaders would lead blind followers—and both would fall.

Never before has wickedness been so openly celebrated, even within the visible church. If a pastor is not preparing his congregation to meet Jesus—through repentance, holiness, and obedience—then it is time to find another ministry.

Salvation is not lost casually—but Scripture clearly teaches that it **can be abandoned.**

CHAPTER ELEVEN

THE POSSIBILITY OF APOSTASY: A BIBLICAL CASE

The doctrine of the perseverance of the saints, articulated by John Calvin and codified in the Fifth Head of Doctrine at the Synod of Dort, teaches that those whom God has effectually called and regenerated will certainly continue in faith until final glorification. Those who appear to fall away were never truly regenerate but possessed only temporary or non-saving faith.

This chapter engages that claim directly. The issue is not whether God preserves His people—Scripture clearly affirms His faithfulness. The question is whether the warning passages describe:

- Hypothetical scenarios,
- Merely external covenant members,
- Or genuinely regenerate believers who face the real possibility of apostasy.

The following texts require careful examination.

1. Hebrews 6:4–6 — Partakers of the Holy Spirit

Hebrews 6 describes individuals who were:

- "Once enlightened,"
- Who "tasted the heavenly gift,"

- Who became "partakers" of the Holy Spirit,
- And who "tasted the good word of God and the powers of the age to come."

The word translated "partakers" (Greek *metochoi*) elsewhere in Hebrews refers to genuine participation (cf. 3:1, 3:14). In 3:14, believers are called "partakers of Christ" if they hold fast their confidence.

Reformed interpreters often argue that "tasted" implies experience short of full salvation. Yet Hebrews 2:9 uses the same verb when it says Christ "tasted death," clearly meaning full participation, not superficial contact.

The description in Hebrews 6 is cumulative and experiential. The text does not signal that these individuals were merely exposed to the covenant community. The force of the warning appears grounded in the reality of what has been experienced.

If the author intended to describe only superficial believers, the language is unusually strong.

2. Hebrews 10:26–29 — Sanctified by the Blood

Hebrews 10 speaks of someone who has counted "the blood of the covenant, wherewith he was sanctified," as unholy.

The verb "sanctified" (Greek *hagiazo*) in Hebrews consistently refers to the redemptive work accomplished by Christ's sacrifice (10:10, 10:14).

Reformed theology often distinguishes between internal regeneration and external covenant membership. Some argue this sanctification refers only to visible church association.

However, the sanctification here is explicitly tied to Christ's blood—the same blood that cleanses the conscience (9:14). The warning concerns deliberate, ongoing sin after receiving the knowledge of the truth.

The severity of the judgment described suggests prior participation in covenant blessing.

3. 2 Peter 2:20–22 — Escaped Through Knowledge of Christ

Peter describes individuals who:

- Escaped the defilements of the world
- Through the "knowledge" (*epignosis*) of the Lord and Savior Jesus Christ
- And then become entangled again

The term translated "knowledge" often refers to full, relational knowledge in Peter's writings (cf. 2 Pet. 1:2–3). The language parallels earlier descriptions of believers escaping corruption through God's promises.

Reformed interpreters sometimes argue this refers to moral reform without regeneration. Yet Peter's language closely resembles conversion terminology elsewhere in the epistle.

He concludes that their latter state is worse than the first—implying a real transition into and out of covenant blessing.

4. John 15:1–6 — Branches "In Me"

In John 15, Jesus declares:

"Every branch in Me that does not bear fruit He takes away."

Throughout John's Gospel, the phrase "in Me" refers to relational union (cf. John 6:56; 14:20). The vine imagery suggests organic connection, not mere proximity.

Reformed theology distinguishes between visible attachment and vital union, arguing that unfruitful branches were never truly regenerate.

Yet the repeated command to "abide" indicates that continuance in that relationship is necessary. The warning reads as genuine, not merely illustrative.

5. Romans 11:17–22 — You Stand by Faith

Paul warns Gentile believers:

"You stand by faith… do not become proud, but fear… otherwise you too will be cut off."

Perseverance is explicitly connected to continued faith. Reformed interpreters often read this corporately rather than individually.

Yet Paul addresses his readers personally: "You stand by faith." The exhortation to fear carries real weight only if the warning is meaningful.

The pattern resembles covenant warnings throughout Scripture—participation in blessing is maintained through continued trust.

6. Reformed Counterarguments Considered

A. The Warnings as Means of Perseverance

Reformed theology argues that warnings are the very means God uses to preserve the elect. They are real warnings, but they ultimately secure perseverance rather than describe a genuine possibility of final loss.

This proposal is theologically coherent. Yet the warning passages themselves do not present apostasy as merely hypothetical. They read as serious cautions addressed to believers.

B. "They Were Never Truly Saved"

Appeal is often made to 1 John 2:19: "They went out from us, but they were not of us."

However, that verse addresses a specific historical situation and does not automatically redefine every warning passage in the New Testament.

The author of Hebrews does not say that those who fall away were never truly among the saved; instead, he urges his readers not to follow that path.

C. Temporary Faith

Some Reformed theologians speak of "temporary" or "non-saving" faith to explain those who appear to believe but later fall away.

The difficulty is that the warning passages themselves do not introduce such distinctions. They describe participation in strong, experiential language without qualification.

7. Covenant Relationship and Conditional Continuance

Throughout Scripture, covenant relationship includes both promise and responsibility. Continued participation in covenant blessing is repeatedly tied to continued faith (cf. Col. 1:23; 1 Cor. 15:2).

This does not deny salvation by grace. It affirms that saving faith is living and persevering.

Apostasy is not momentary doubt or spiritual struggle. It is the decisive and persistent repudiation of Christ.

Grace enables perseverance. Yet Scripture repeatedly calls believers to continue, to abide, and to endure.

The warning passages examined—Hebrews 6, Hebrews 10, 2 Peter 2, John 15, and Romans 11—use language that naturally reads as describing genuine participation in salvific realities followed by the possibility of decisive rejection.

While the Reformed doctrine of perseverance seeks to safeguard the certainty of God's promises, these texts present warnings that appear covenantally real rather than merely rhetorical.

The biblical tension should not be prematurely resolved.

The call of Scripture is not passive security, but persevering faith.

CHAPTER TWELVE

COMMON OBJECTIONS TO CONDITIONAL SECURITY

The doctrine of conditional security raises serious questions. For many believers, the idea that perseverance matters can feel unsettling. Some fear that such a view undermines grace, weakens assurance, or contradicts key promises of Scripture.

These concerns deserve careful and respectful consideration.

This chapter addresses the most common objections to conditional security and evaluates them in light of the full counsel of Scripture.

Objection 1: "You Are Teaching Salvation by Works"

Perhaps the most frequent accusation is that conditional security makes salvation dependent upon human effort. If perseverance is necessary, critics argue, then salvation becomes something we maintain through works rather than receive by grace.

This objection misunderstands the distinction between earning salvation and continuing in faith.

The New Testament consistently teaches that salvation is initiated by grace through faith (Ephesians 2:8–9). No one earns justification. No one merits redemption. Christ alone accomplishes salvation.

Yet Scripture also teaches that genuine faith produces obedience and endurance. James writes, "Faith without works is dead" (James 2:17). Jesus declares, "He that shall endure unto the end, the same shall be saved" (Matthew 24:13). Paul exhorts believers to continue in the faith, grounded and settled (Colossians 1:23).

These passages do not present works as the cause of salvation but as the evidence of living faith.

Grace is not opposed to effort; it is opposed to earning. Perseverance is not self-reliance but continued reliance upon the grace that first saved us.

Conditional security does not say, "Work hard enough to remain saved."
It says, "Remain in Christ, and His grace will sustain you."

That is covenant faithfulness, not legalism.

Objection 2: "Doesn't Romans 8 Teach Absolute Security?"

Romans 8:38–39 declares that nothing shall be able to separate us from the love of God which is in Christ Jesus our Lord.

This is a powerful promise of assurance.

But notice what Paul lists: death, life, angels, principalities, powers, things present, things to come. These are external forces.

Paul affirms that no external power can forcibly separate a believer from Christ.

He does not address the question of whether a person may depart through persistent unbelief or hardened rebellion.

Indeed, the same apostle later warns believers: "Be not highminded, but fear… for if God spared not the natural branches, take heed lest he also spare not thee" (Romans 11:20–21).

Romans 8 teaches the security of those who remain in Christ. It does not nullify the warnings given elsewhere in Scripture.

Objection 3: "No One Shall Pluck Them Out of My Hand"

In John 10:28–29, Jesus says:

"And I give unto them eternal life; and they shall never perish, neither shall any man pluck them out of my hand."

This promise is precious and true.

But observe how Jesus describes His sheep:

"My sheep hear my voice, and I know them, and they follow me" (John 10:27).

The promise of security is given to those who continue hearing and following.

The text assures us that no external enemy can snatch Christ's sheep from His hand. It does not address a sheep that ceases to follow.

Scripture must be read in harmony. The same Gospel records Jesus saying, "Abide in me… If a man abide not in me, he is cast forth as a branch" (John 15:4–6).

The promises of protection and the warnings of departure coexist in the teaching of Christ.

Objection 4: "This View Destroys Assurance"

Some argue that conditional security leaves believers in constant anxiety, uncertain of their salvation.

But biblical assurance is rooted in present faith, not merely in a past event.

John writes, "These things have I written unto you that believe on the name of the Son of God; that ye may know that ye have eternal life" (1 John 5:13).

Assurance belongs to those who believe — present tense.

A believer walking in repentance, obedience, and faith may have strong confidence in Christ. The call to perseverance does not eliminate assurance; it defines it properly. False assurance rests in a memory. True assurance rests in a living relationship. Conditional security removes presumption, not peace.

Objection 5: "If They Fall Away, They Were Never Truly Saved"

This argument frequently appeals to 1 John 2:19:

"They went out from us, but they were not of us."

Certainly, some who profess faith were never truly converted. Scripture acknowledges false disciples and superficial belief.

But this verse cannot be used as a universal explanation for every instance of apostasy.

Other passages describe individuals who were:

- Sanctified by the blood of the covenant (Hebrews 10:29)
- Partakers of the Holy Ghost (Hebrews 6:4)
- Escaped the pollutions of the world through the knowledge of the Lord (2 Peter 2:20)

These descriptions appear to go beyond mere outward association.

The New Testament contains both categories:
those who were never genuinely converted and those who genuinely participated and later fell away.

We must allow Scripture to speak with its full weight.

Holding the Balance

The purpose of conditional security is not to weaken grace but to take Scripture seriously.

God is faithful, and Christ is sufficient. The Spirit empowers endurance. Yet the New Testament repeatedly calls believers to continue, abide, hold fast, and endure.

To affirm perseverance as necessary is not to diminish grace. It is to recognize that salvation is relational, covenantal, and lived. The warnings are not theoretical. They are pastoral. They do not undermine assurance. They protect it. Salvation is secure in Christ. But Scripture consistently calls believers to remain in Him.

CHAPTER THIRTEEN

PASTORAL AND ECCLESIAL IMPLICATIONS

Doctrinal debates are often treated as abstract exercises. Words are parsed, positions defended, systems compared. But the doctrine of eternal security—or conditional security—is not merely academic.

It shapes how people live, how pastors preach, and it shapes how churches disciple. Ultimately, it shapes how believers think about eternity.

This discussion is not about winning theological arguments. It is about whether the church takes the warnings of Scripture seriously.

The Danger of Presumption

One of the gravest spiritual dangers in any age is presumption.

Presumption says: "I made a decision years ago. I am safe, no matter how I live now."

The New Testament never encourages this mindset.

Instead, it repeatedly exhorts believers to:

- Continue in the faith (Colossians 1:23)
- Examine themselves (2 Corinthians 13:5)
- Work out their salvation with fear and trembling (Philippians 2:12)
- Take heed lest they fall (1 Corinthians 10:12)

These are not warnings directed at pagans. They are directed at believers.

When the possibility of falling away is removed in theory, vigilance often weakens in practice. The call to holiness softens. The urgency of repentance fades.

Conditional security does not create fear. It restores seriousness.

It reminds believers that salvation is not a casual affiliation but a living covenant.

The Rise of Casual Christianity

In many modern contexts, conversion is reduced to a moment.

A prayer.
A raised hand.
A signed card.

While God can certainly use decisive moments, the New Testament consistently presents salvation as a new birth that produces transformation.

Jesus said, "By their fruits ye shall know them" (Matthew 7:20).

The apostles spoke of a faith that works by love (Galatians 5:6), of obedience from the heart (Romans 6:17), and of enduring to the end (Hebrews 3:14).

When eternal security is detached from perseverance, it can unintentionally encourage a truncated gospel—one that emphasizes justification while minimizing sanctification.

The result is not theological clarity but spiritual complacency.

This is not to say that every proponent of eternal security promotes carelessness. Many do not. Many preach holiness vigorously.

But ideas have consequences. If believers are taught that final salvation is guaranteed irrespective of continued faith, some will inevitably interpret that as permission to drift. The New Testament does not speak this way.

Shepherd Accountability

The doctrine we teach affects the souls entrusted to us.

In Ezekiel, God warns the watchman that failure to sound the alarm carries consequences (Ezekiel 3:18–21).

The New Testament echoes this seriousness. Leaders are told they will give account (Hebrews 13:17). Teachers are warned of stricter judgment (James 3:1).

If Scripture contains genuine warnings about falling away, then those warnings must be preached—not softened, not explained away, not dismissed as purely hypothetical.

A shepherd who never warns is not being kind. He may be comforting people into danger.

Balanced teaching affirms both:

- The sufficiency of Christ
- The necessity of endurance

Both are biblical.

Grace Properly Understood

Some fear that emphasizing perseverance diminishes grace. In reality, it highlights grace.

Grace does not merely pardon sin. It trains us.

"For the grace of God that bringeth salvation hath appeared… teaching us that, denying ungodliness and worldly lusts, we should live soberly, righteously, and godly" (Titus 2:11–12).

Grace is not passive. It is transformative.

To continue in faith is not to move beyond grace—it is to remain under its influence.

The Spirit who regenerates also convicts, empowers, and preserves. But Scripture never portrays that preserving work as something that overrides persistent rebellion.

Grace invites cooperation.

It does not eliminate responsibility.

Assurance Without Arrogance

A healthy church culture cultivates assurance—but not arrogance.

Believers should have confidence in Christ and should rest in His promises. They should rejoice in His finished work. But they should not presume upon mercy while neglecting obedience.

There is a profound difference between confidence and complacency. Confidence says:

"Christ is faithful; I trust Him daily." Complacency says: "I am safe; nothing I do now matters."

The New Testament consistently encourages the first and warns against the second.

A Call to Watchfulness

Jesus frequently used the language of watchfulness.

"Watch therefore" (Matthew 24:42).

"Take heed" (Luke 21:34).

"Abide in me" (John 15:4).

These are relational commands. They are not threats designed to paralyze believers. They are invitations to remain alert, faithful, and dependent. A doctrine that removes watchfulness from the Christian life risks dulling spiritual sensitivity.

The early church did not preach despair. They preached endurance. They expected believers to remain faithful. They believed grace was sufficient—but not automatic.

The Heart of the Matter

Ultimately, this discussion returns to a simple question:

What does Scripture teach?

If Scripture presents salvation as a dynamic relationship requiring perseverance, then that is what must be taught—gently, clearly, and faithfully.

If Scripture contains real warnings addressed to real believers, then those warnings must be honored.

This is not about insecurity.

It is about integrity.

The church must hold together what Scripture holds together:

The faithfulness of God
and
The call to endure.

When those truths remain in balance, believers are neither terrified nor careless.

They are watchful. They are grateful. And they remain in Christ.

CHAPTER FOURTEEN
THE REALITY OF FINAL JUDGMENT

Throughout this book, we have examined the question of perseverance and the possibility of falling away. We have considered the promises of assurance and the warnings of Scripture. We have evaluated the testimony of the early church and addressed common objections.

Now we must consider what ultimately stands behind those warnings:

The reality of final judgment.

Christian theology does not end with conversion. It ends with accountability before God.

Scripture speaks with remarkable clarity on this point. "It is appointed unto men once to die, but after this the judgment" (Hebrews 9:27, KJV). Death is not the end of moral responsibility. It is the threshold to divine evaluation.

Every human being will stand before God.

Paul writes, "For we must all appear before the judgment seat of Christ; that every one may receive the things done in his body, according to that he hath done, whether it be good or bad" (2 Corinthians 5:10, KJV).

Judgment is not an abstract doctrine. It is a future certainty.

The Certainty of Judgment

From Genesis to Revelation, Scripture affirms that God will judge the living and the dead. The final chapters of the Bible describe a great white throne before which the dead are judged "according to their works" (Revelation 20:12, KJV). Those whose names are not found written in the Book of Life are cast into the lake of fire (Revelation 20:15).

These passages are not poetic exaggerations. They are sober declarations.

Jesus Himself spoke often of final separation. In Matthew 25:46, He describes two eternal outcomes: "And these shall go away into everlasting punishment: but the righteous into life eternal." The duration of both destinies is presented in parallel terms. Eternal life and eternal punishment stand side by side.

Final judgment is not inconsistent with grace. It is consistent with justice.

The same Scriptures that proclaim salvation by grace also affirm that God will judge in righteousness.

Eternal Separation

Scripture describes the fate of the unrepentant not merely in terms of punishment, but separation. Paul writes that those who "obey not the gospel of our Lord Jesus Christ" shall be punished "with everlasting destruction from the presence of the Lord, and from the glory of his power" (2 Thessalonians 1:8–9, KJV).

The essence of judgment is exclusion from the presence of God.

This is not presented to provoke fear for its own sake. It is presented as reality. The gospel offers reconciliation because separation is otherwise certain.

Throughout this book, we have asked whether Scripture teaches that a person who once believed can never ultimately fall away. If the warning passages are genuine, then the consequence of final unbelief cannot be trivial.

If perseverance matters, then its absence has eternal significance.

Apostasy and Its End

Several warning passages connect falling away with severe consequences. Hebrews 10:26–27 states that if we sin willfully after receiving the knowledge of the truth, "there remaineth no more sacrifice for sins, but a certain fearful looking for of judgment."

Second Peter 2:20–21 describes those who have escaped the pollutions of the world through the knowledge of the Lord and Savior Jesus Christ, yet become entangled again. It concludes that "the latter end is worse with them than the beginning."

These texts are not included in Scripture accidentally. They function as warnings precisely because something serious is at stake.

If apostasy were impossible, such language would lose its force.

The New Testament consistently treats perseverance not as an optional enhancement to salvation, but as integral to it. "We are made partakers of Christ, if we hold the beginning of our confidence stedfast unto the end" (Hebrews 3:14, KJV).

The conditional language cannot be dismissed lightly.

Why Warnings Are Acts of Mercy

Warnings in Scripture are not threats designed to produce anxiety. They are acts of mercy designed to prevent destruction.

In Ezekiel 3:18–19, God tells the prophet that if he fails to warn the wicked, their blood will be required at his hand. But if he warns them and they do not turn, he has delivered his own soul.

The purpose of warning is preservation.

Similarly, Paul told the Ephesian elders that he was innocent of the blood of all men because he had not shunned to declare the whole counsel of God (Acts 20:26–27). His warning ministry was an expression of love.

A gospel that includes promise but excludes warning is incomplete.

The New Testament does not pit assurance against accountability. It holds them together.

Assurance Without Presumption

The reality of judgment should not produce panic in the faithful believer. Scripture consistently affirms that those who abide in Christ may have confidence. "There is therefore now no condemnation to them which are in Christ Jesus" (Romans 8:1, KJV).

But notice the phrase: "in Christ Jesus."

Salvation is secure in Him.

The warnings do not undermine assurance; they define its boundaries. They call believers to remain where safety is found.

The doctrine of perseverance, rightly understood, does not minimize judgment. It emphasizes God's preserving grace. The doctrine of conditional security, rightly understood, does not minimize grace. It emphasizes the necessity of continued faith.

Both positions must reckon with the reality that judgment is final and irreversible.

What Is at Stake

This discussion is not academic. It concerns eternal destiny.

If Scripture teaches that believers must endure, then endurance matters. If Scripture warns that falling away results in judgment, those warnings must not be softened.

The purpose of this chapter is not to instill fear, but clarity.

Eternity is real. Judgment is certain. Christ is sufficient. The call of Scripture is simple and consistent:

Abide in Him.
Continue in the faith.
Hold fast your confidence.

The reality of final judgment does not diminish grace. It magnifies its value. It reminds us that salvation is precious, not casual. It calls us to seriously continue without despair and vigilance without panic.

The church must preach both hope and warning.

To proclaim Christ faithfully is to declare that He saves completely — and that those who remain in Him will share in His eternal life.

The final word of Scripture is not destruction. It is restoration for those who overcome.

But overcoming implies perseverance.

And perseverance matters.

CONCLUSION

In 2026, an estimated 174,000 to 175,000 people die every day, that's 7,250 per hour, 121 per minute, and 2 per second[25]. Every death represents an eternal soul, and every moment presents a choice.

If you hold to the belief that salvation can never be lost, consider carefully what Scripture teaches:

1. Jesus is coming for a church without spot or blemish (Ephesians 5:27, KJV).
2. Not everyone who calls Him "Lord, Lord" will enter heaven (Matthew 7:21–23, KJV).
3. Believers are commanded to work out their own salvation with fear and trembling (Philippians 2:12, KJV).
4. We are commanded to live holy (1 Peter 1:16; Leviticus 11:44, KJV).
5. Names can be blotted out of the Book of Life (Revelation 3:5, KJV).

To ignore these warnings is to tread on dangerous ground.

Every generation of believers faces the same question: Will we hold together what Scripture requires: to be faithful in God and to heed the call to endure?

Throughout this book we have examined the doctrine commonly called "Once Saved, Always Saved." We have explored its development

---

[25] StatisticsTimes.com

within Reformed theology, considered the testimony of the early church, evaluated key warning passages, and have addressed objections.

At every turn, one truth has remained constant: Scripture speaks both assurance and warning.

It assures us that Christ is sufficient. Nothing external can overpower His saving grace. Those who trust Him may rest in His promises.

But it also warns believers not to drift. It warns against hardened unbelief. It warns that perseverance matters.

These warnings are not accidental. They are pastoral safeguards.

Salvation Is Secure in Christ

Let this be stated plainly: Salvation is not fragile, and Christ is not weak. Further, God is not unreliable. The cross was not insufficient. Those who remain in Christ may have deep and settled assurance. The believer walking in repentance, faith, and obedience need not live in fear. The Shepherd is faithful. His grace is sufficient. His Spirit empowers endurance.

Yet Scripture consistently describes salvation as relational.

- Jesus says, "Abide in me" (John 15:4).
- The writer of Hebrews says, "Hold fast" (Hebrews 3:14).
- And Paul says, "Continue in the faith" (Colossians 1:23).

These are not calls to self-reliance. They are invitations to remain in dependence.

The Danger of Presumption

If there is a spiritual threat in our time, it is not excessive fear. It is presumption.

Presumption says: "I once believed. That is enough."

But Scripture speaks of a living faith. A continuing faith. A persevering faith. The New Testament does not teach that a past profession guarantees future glory irrespective of present reality. It calls believers to endure - not in panic, but in watchfulness.

To ignore these warnings is not confidence. It is carelessness.

A Word to the Complacent

If you are resting solely on a decision made years ago while living in deliberate disobedience, this book calls you to examine yourself.

Return. Repent. Remain.

Grace remains available. But grace must not be presumed upon. God's mercy is vast. Scripture never encourages spiritual indifference.

A Word to the Faithful

If you are walking in repentance, trusting Christ, seeking holiness, and grieving over sin, this book is not written to unsettle you. It is written to strengthen you.

Your endurance does not rest on your strength alone. It rests on the sustaining grace of God. Continue to abide in Christ. Continue to trust. Continue to obey. The same grace that saved you will sustain you — as you remain in Him.

A Word to Shepherds

Pastors and teachers bear weighty responsibility. We must preach the promises. We must also preach the warnings. We must comfort the afflicted. We must also awaken the drifting. A balanced gospel includes both.

Ezekiel was called to sound the alarm. The apostles were called to exhort the church daily.
So must we.

Ezekiel 3:18–21 (KJV) reminds us that warning the wayward is not optional but necessary. God holds His servants accountable to speak truthfully and faithfully.

The Final Appeal

This book does not claim to settle every theological nuance. But it does insist that Scripture calls believers to perseverance. Salvation is a gift of grace. But grace does not eliminate the call to remain.

Therefore: Remain in Christ. Continue in the faith. Hold fast your confidence. Walk in humility, and endure in hope. God is faithful. Let us be faithful in response.

God is calling His shepherds to prepare the flock for Christ's return— to teach holiness, obedience, and faithful service. Ezekiel 3:18–21 (KJV) makes this responsibility clear:

"When I say unto the wicked, 'Thou shalt surely die,' and you give him no warning, nor speak to warn him from his wicked way, that man shall die in his iniquity; but his blood I will require at your hand. Yet if you warn the wicked, and he does not turn from his

wickedness, he shall die in his iniquity; but you have delivered your soul. Likewise, when a righteous man turns from his righteousness and commits iniquity, and I lay a stumbling block before him, he shall die... Nevertheless, if you warn the righteous man, that he sin not, and he does not sin, he shall surely live, because he was warned; also you have delivered your soul."

This passage underscores two truths: God holds us accountable, and we are called to warn and guide others. The choices you make today echo into eternity.

EPILOGUE

A PASTORAL APPEAL - REMAIN IN CHRIST

Did the Early Church Believe "Once Saved, Always Saved"?

Many modern Christians assume that "Once Saved, Always Saved" has always been the church's belief. But when we examine the earliest Christian writers—those closest to the apostles—we find something different.

They did not treat salvation as a guaranteed possession secured by a past decision. They spoke of salvation as a life to be lived, a race to be finished, a faith to be guarded:

- Ignatius warned believers not merely to be called Christians, but to live as such.
- Polycarp said resurrection comes if we do God's will.
- Irenaeus warned that disobedient believers could forfeit sonship.
- Tertullian treated post-baptismal sin as spiritually dangerous.
- Origen read biblical warnings about falling away as real.

Even Augustine, often cited to defend eternal security, distinguished between believers who receive grace and those who receive the gift of perseverance. Not all who begin finish.

The early church did not preach anxiety. They preached vigilance. They did not deny grace. They insisted that grace must be continued in.

Scripture repeatedly warns believers:

"Take heed… lest there be in any of you an evil heart of unbelief, in departing from the living God." (Hebrews 3:12, KJV)

The early Christians read those warnings plainly.

The takeaway is not fear—but faithfulness.

- Salvation is secure for those in Christ.
- Scripture calls us to remain in Him.

DOCTRINAL STATEMENT SUMMARY

This book affirms:

- The full inspiration and authority of Scripture
- Salvation by grace alone through faith alone
- The necessity of repentance and new birth
- The reality of genuine conversion
- The believer's call to perseverance
- The possibility of apostasy through deliberate, persistent unbelief
- Final salvation for those who endure in faith to the end

This book rejects:

- The teaching that a past profession of faith guarantees final salvation irrespective of continued faith
- The claim that all warning passages are merely hypothetical
- Any theology that removes the seriousness of biblical exhortations to endure

APPENDIX

PATRISTIC TERMINOLOGY AND SOTERIOLOGICAL ASSUMPTIONS

To avoid anachronism, several key terms must be clarified:

1. Regeneration

- o In early Christianity, regeneration was ordinarily associated with baptism. It did not function as a purely internal, forensic category detached from ecclesial life.

2. Salvation

- o Salvation was often described as:
    - Illumination
    - Participation
    - Adoption
    - Deification (theosis)
- o These were dynamic realities, not merely legal declarations.

3. Perseverance

- o Perseverance was understood morally and covenantally, not as metaphysical inevitability. Exhortations to endure assume that believers must continue responding to grace.

4. Apostasy

- ○ Apostasy was not treated as loss of rewards but as real spiritual ruin. The seriousness of post-baptismal penitential discipline in the early church confirms this assumption.

METHODOLOGICAL NOTE

This book presents a historical-theoloigcal perspective emphasizing perseverance and responsible faith. Interpretations of Scripture and patristic writings reflect one scholarly reading and are intended to guide practical application, not to settle all theological debates. Readers are encouraged to consult the Bible and primary sources for study and discernment.

BIBLIOGRAPHY

Primary Sources

- Athanasius of Alexandria. *On the Incarnation*. Translated by John Behr. Yonkers, NY: St. Vladimir's Seminary Press, 2011.

- Augustine of Hippo. *On the Gift of Perseverance*. In *Nicene and Post-Nicene Fathers, First Series*, Vol. 5. Edited by Philip Schaff. Buffalo, NY: Christian Literature Publishing, 1887.

- ———. *On Rebuke and Grace*. In *Nicene and Post-Nicene Fathers, First Series*, Vol. 5. Edited by Philip Schaff. Buffalo, NY: Christian Literature Publishing, 1887.

- Clement of Rome. *The First Epistle of Clement*. In *The Apostolic Fathers*. Translated by J. B. Lightfoot and J. R. Harmer. Grand Rapids: Baker, 1989.

- Ignatius of Antioch. *Letters*. In *The Apostolic Fathers*. Translated by J. B. Lightfoot and J. R. Harmer. Grand Rapids: Baker, 1989.

- Irenaeus of Lyons. *Against Heresies*. In *Ante-Nicene Fathers*, Vol. 1. Buffalo, NY: Christian Literature Publishing, 1885.

- Origen. *Homilies on Ezekiel*. Translated by Thomas P. Scheck. Washington, DC: Catholic University of America Press, 2010.

- Polycarp of Smyrna. *Epistle to the Philippians*. In *The Apostolic Fathers*. Translated by J. B. Lightfoot and J. R. Harmer. Grand Rapids: Baker, 1989.

- Tertullian. *On Modesty*. In *Ante-Nicene Fathers*, Vol. 4. Buffalo, NY: Christian Literature Publishing, 1885.

Reformed Sources

- John Calvin. *Institutes of the Christian Religion*. Edited by John T. McNeill. Translated by Ford Lewis Battles. 2 vols. Philadelphia: Westminster Press, 1960.
- Synod of Dort. *The Canons of Dort*, 1619.

Secondary Sources

- Bray, Gerald. *God Has Spoken: A History of Christian Theology*. Wheaton, IL: Crossway, 2014.
- Hall, Christopher A. *Reading Scripture with the Church Fathers*. Downers Grove, IL: IVP Academic, 1998.
- Jenson, Robert Louis. *The Triune Identity*. Philadelphia: Fortress Press, 1982.

ABOUT THE AUTHOR

Anthony V. Johnson, often called a "Renaissance Man," was born at Fort Benning Army Base, home to prestigious military schools and elite units. Influenced by his father, a Lieutenant Colonel and decorated Vietnam veteran laid to rest at Arlington National Cemetery, Anthony developed a lifelong appreciation for discipline, service, and excellence.

His passion for music began at age seven in Paris, France, and by 14, he was performing in jazz nightclubs. At 17, he joined the Army, earning the nickname "the Singing Corporal" for his cadence calling, later promoted to Sergeant, and served as an Infantry Squad Leader and member of the U.S. Army Mounted Color Guard & Drill Team. He graduated from the rigorous Combat Leader's School at Camp Red Devil and earned the esteemed Expert Infantryman's Badge (EIB).

Anthony's professional journey spans music, law, health physics, and leadership coaching. He performed across Europe and the U.S. in theater musicals, big bands, and various recording acts. As founder of **Quiet Authority™**, he coaches professionals in persuasive communication under pressure. He has also served as a Trial Lawyer and Senior Health Physics Technician at U.S. nuclear facilities, overseeing radiation safety, emergency response, and regulatory compliance.

Anthony holds an A.S. in Business Administration, a B.A. in English, and a Doctor of Jurisprudence. He continues his musical ministry in worship teams across American, Brazilian, and Spanish churches and organized **"A Gathering of the Nations"**, uniting global ministries in multilingual worship. His work in the Spiritual Rights Movement earned him the **Global Leadership Award** from "I Change Nations."

Passionate about aviation, scuba diving, martial arts, travel, and foreign missions, Anthony brings a diverse and adventurous perspective to every pursuit. He can be reached at:

contact@anthonyvjohnson.com.